Original title:

Joyful Bliss

Author: Clement Portlander

ISBN HARDBACK: 978-9916-88-160-6

ISBN PAPERBACK: 978-9916-88-161-3

A Canvas of Lighthearted Moments

Laughter dances in the air,
Colors bright, without a care.
Joyful whispers fill the night,
Painting hearts with pure delight.

In every smile, a story blooms,
As starlit dreams disperse the glooms.
Together here, we lift our gaze,
In this love, forever stays.

Sparkling Eyes and Genuine Grins

Eyes that twinkle, hearts that sing,
Moments shared in everything.
With genuine grins, we embrace the day,
In the warmth of friendship, we find our way.

Simple joys and playful jest,
In each encounter, we feel blessed.
Together we chase the fading light,
In laughter's dance, our souls take flight.

The Magic of Serene Belonging

In quiet corners, bonds are sewn,
Among the whispers, love is grown.
Familiar laughter, gentle touch,
In this haven, we find so much.

Wrapped in warmth, we share our dreams,
In tranquil moments, life redeems.
No need for words, our hearts do speak,
In this embrace, we find the meek.

The Essence of Childlike Wonder

In fields of green, we run and play,
As butterflies dance, we lose our way.
Every flower holds a secret bright,
In innocent hearts, the world feels right.

With open eyes, we chase the sky,
In every cloud, we learn to fly.
The universe sings in playful tones,
In childlike wonder, we feel at home.

Laughter Painted on the Canvas of Life

In the gallery of time, we smile,
Bright colors burst, they linger awhile.
Every chuckle, every cheer,
Brush strokes vibrant, memories clear.

With each moment, joy unfolds,
Adventurous tales that life beholds.
Whispers of laughter fill the air,
A masterpiece crafted with care.

A Symphony of Sweet Reminiscence

Notes of laughter play through the years,
Melodies soft, they calm our fears.
In the silence, echoes hum,
A symphony for all that's come.

Each chord dances, a gentle sway,
Carrying memories held at bay.
In every pause, a story beats,
A harmony of life that repeats.

Delightful Daydreams in Pastel Shades

Whispers of magic in the sky,
Pastel dreams that flutter by.
Clouds of cotton, soft and light,
Painted hues in morning's right.

Children laughing, hearts so free,
Colors swirl in jubilee.
Every sigh a breeze that flows,
In our hearts, the warmth just grows.

Charms of the Carefree Imagination

In a world where wishes soar,
Imagination opens doors.
Unicorns and castles bright,
Magic dances in the night.

With every thought, the skies expand,
Crafting stories, hand in hand.
The careless spirit takes to flight,
Spinning dreams into the light.

When Dreams Take Flight

Upon the wings of night we soar,
In whispered winds, we crave for more.
With every star that lights our way,
We chase the dawn of a brand new day.

In realms where wishes softly blend,
We find the courage to transcend.
With hearts alight, through shadows we roam,
For in our dreams, we find our home.

The Color of Unburdened Souls

In fields where blossoms freely sway,
We dance together, come what may.
Each shade a story, bright and true,
Unfettered hearts, in skies so blue.

With laughter shared and kindness spread,
We paint the world, where hope is fed.
Through every hue, our spirits sing,
The color of love in every spring.

Savoring Sweet Surprises

In moments paused, we taste the day,
Like honey dripped in sun's soft ray.
Each smile a gift, a treasure to hold,
A story sweet, waiting to be told.

With every glance, new wonders unfold,
In simple joys, our hearts grow bold.
The spice of life, the warmth of cheer,
In sweet surprises, we find our dear.

Heartstrings Touched by Sunbeams

As morning breaks and shadows fade,
We feel the warmth that love has made.
With every glance, a spark ignites,
In sun-kissed moments, pure delights.

Through gentle rays, our spirits mend,
In laughter shared, our souls transcend.
Heartstrings play a melody bright,
Touched softly by the morning light.

Celebration in Every Breath

In the morning light we rise,
With laughter painting the skies,
Each moment a treasure to hold,
In our hearts, stories unfold.

With every step, a cheer resounds,
Joy and love in leaps and bounds,
We dance to the rhythm so bright,
Celebrating life, pure delight.

The air is filled with vibrant tunes,
As we sway beneath the moons,
Grateful for the chance to see,
The beauty in life's simple spree.

Symphony of Cheerful Echoes

Whispers of joy fill the air,
A symphony beyond compare,
Each laugh a note, a sweet embrace,
In the heart, we find our place.

The sunbeams dance on our skin,
As melodies rise from within,
With every heartbeat, we unite,
Creating harmony, pure light.

Voices blend, creating art,
Each echo plays its vital part,
Together we weave a tale,
A celebration that will not pale.

Glimmers of Pure Contentment

In quiet moments, peace we find,
The gentle whispers of the mind,
A tranquil heart, so full of grace,
Glimmers of joy in every space.

Through valleys low and mountains high,
We savor life as time goes by,
In simple things, our spirits soar,
Contentment at our very core.

Raindrops fall like nature's song,
Where we belong, we are strong,
Each breath a spark of what could be,
In the realm of serenity.

A Garden of Grinning Flowers

In the garden where smiles bloom,
Colors chase away the gloom,
Petals laugh and sway with cheer,
Every blossom whispers near.

With sunshine casting golden rays,
We revel in the joyous days,
Nature's palette, bright and bold,
Stories in each bloom retold.

Among the leaves, our spirits dance,
In this realm of sweet romance,
A garden filled with laughter's power,
In every stem, a grinning flower.

Welcoming Waves of Delight

The ocean whispers to the shore,
Softly urging hearts to soar.
Sun-kissed breezes fill the air,
Bringing joy without a care.

Seagulls cry above the foam,
Tides invite us to come home.
Shells and treasures line the sand,
Nature's gifts, a painter's hand.

Children laugh, their spirits bright,
Chasing shadows in the light.
Footprints trace our happy dance,
Every moment, a sweet chance.

As the day fades into night,
Stars ignite, a wondrous sight.
In this place of blissful grace,
We find our peace, our sacred space.

A Mosaic of Grateful Hearts

Colors blend in perfect hue,
Gratitude shapes all we do.
In this patchwork of dreams desired,
Each thread woven, love inspired.

Every face tells a story true,
Bonded by moments, old and new.
Hands held tight, no fear to part,
Together we create, heart to heart.

Through storms faced and tears we shed,
Hope's gentle light is never dead.
In every corner of this place,
The warmth of kindness we embrace.

A garden blooms, love's sweet refrain,
In joy and sorrow, growth from pain.
Grateful hearts pulse side by side,
In this mosaic, we abide.

Dance of the Carefree Spirits

Underneath the summer sky,
Joyful laughter fills the high.
Feet that twirl on vibrant grass,
Moments swift, we let them pass.

Windy whispers guide our way,
In the sun, we choose to play.
Carefree souls, we're wild and free,
Chasing dreams with energy.

Colors swirl, a vibrant trance,
Lost in rhythm, join the dance.
Every heartbeat sings a tune,
Beneath the sun, beneath the moon.

As the stars begin to gleam,
We will dance, forever dream.
In this space, we find our song,
With every step, we all belong.

Threads of Ecstatic Whispers

In the quiet of the night,
Echoes dance in soft moonlight.
Whispers weave through ancient trees,
Carried on the gentle breeze.

Secrets shared by stars above,
Wrapped in warmth, a world of love.
Every sigh, a story spun,
Tales of loss, and joy, and fun.

Feel the heartbeat in the calm,
Nature's voice, a soothing balm.
Threads connect us, near and far,
Binding dreams like a shooting star.

In this sacred, silent space,
Whispers linger, hearts embrace.
Ecstatic joys and tender sighs,
Threads of whispers fill the skies.

Sunlit Mornings and Warm Embraces

Golden rays break through the night,
Kissing earth with soft delight.
Whispers of a gentle breeze,
Awaken dreams among the trees.

Laughter dances in the air,
Joyous hearts, no room for despair.
Every moment, pure and bright,
Melodies of morning light.

Together we will share this day,
Chasing shadows far away.
With warm embraces, we ignite,
A world wrapped in golden light.

Rhapsody of Radiant Smiles

In the garden, where we meet,
Sun-kissed blooms and laughter sweet.
Every glance, a spark divine,
Your radiant smile, forever mine.

Moments wrapped in tender grace,
Shining warmth in our embrace.
Hearts in tune, a vibrant song,
In this rhapsody, we belong.

Every smile, a bursting cheer,
In your presence, skies are clear.
Together weaving dreams so bright,
In the magic of the night.

Tapestry of Elation

Threads of joy, stitched with care,
Each one woven, light to share.
Colors dance upon the loom,
Creating beauty, chasing gloom.

Every laugh, a thread of gold,
Stories shared, beautifully told.
In the fabric of our days,
Elation shines in countless ways.

Richly woven memories stay,
Binding us in love's array.
With each moment we embrace,
Our tapestry, a sacred space.

The Lightness of Being

Floating gently like a feather,
In this world, we are together.
Moments cherished, light as air,
In your gaze, I find my care.

Whispers of the softest breeze,
Bringing peace, our hearts at ease.
With every heartbeat, love we glean,
In the lightness of our dream.

Soaring high above the ground,
In this joy, we both are found.
Let us dance beneath the sky,
In this sweetness, you and I.

A Festival of Glee

Laughter spills upon the ground,
Joyful faces all around.
Children dance in vibrant light,
Hearts are lifted, spirits bright.

Balloons drift into the sky,
Wishes whispered, passing by.
Songs of happiness do play,
In this festival of day.

Colorful booths and treats abound,
Sweet aromas fill the ground.
Smiles exchanged with every glance,
A world aglow, a merry dance.

As the sun begins to fade,
Magic lingers, never strayed.
In the warmth, friendships grow,
A festival of joy in tow.

Cascades of Enchantment

Waterfalls in moonlit grace,
Nature's beauty, soft embrace.
Whispers echo through the trees,
Gentle breezes, calming ease.

Stars reflect in tranquil streams,
Where time pauses, lost in dreams.
Fairy lights twinkle and glow,
In the night, a soft tableau.

Misty paths that weave and wind,
Adventures waiting to unwind.
Footsteps light on dampened ground,
In this magic, peace is found.

As shadows dance with evening light,
Hearts are lifted, spirits bright.
In the quiet, wonder grows,
Cascades of enchantment flows.

Luminous Laughter

Sunrise spills its golden hue,
Morning whispers, fresh and new.
Children giggle in the sun,
Every moment, joy begun.

Playful shadows stretch and sway,
Chasing dreams throughout the day.
Laughter rings through open air,
A melody beyond compare.

As twilight drapes its velvet cloak,
Stories shared with every joke.
In each heartbeat, magic glows,
Luminous light in laughter flows.

Fingers intertwined so tight,
With friends gathered, hearts take flight.
In this warmth, we find our place,
Luminous laughter, purest grace.

The Color of Contentment

Beneath the shade of ancient trees,
Whispers dance upon the breeze.
Fields of gold and skies of blue,
Nature wraps us in its view.

Moments treasured, calm and still,
Every breath, a soothing thrill.
Time slows down, a gentle pace,
In tranquil thoughts, we find our space.

Evening paints the world in hues,
Softest reds and calming blues.
In the dusk, all cares retreat,
The color of contentment sweet.

With hands held close, we sit and sigh,
Underneath the vast, wide sky.
In this bliss, our hearts grow bright,
The color of love, warm and light.

Boundless Grins

In fields where laughter flows,
Bright faces dance and glow.
Joy spills from every seam,
Life's a never-ending dream.

With every step we take,
We weave a joyful wake.
The world feels light and free,
In boundless harmony.

Under the sky so wide,
Together we reside.
With hearts that beat as one,
Our laughter weighs a ton.

When shadows start to creep,
We still joyfully leap.
For love's a vital spark,
That shines within the dark.

Twilight of Elation

As day begins to fade,
Soft hues of joy cascade.
In twilight's gentle light,
We find our hearts take flight.

Whispers float on the breeze,
A world of lovely ease.
With every star that shines,
Our laughter intertwines.

In the dusk's warm embrace,
We gather, face to face.
Sharing stories so bright,
Under the cloak of night.

Elation fills the air,
In moments we all share.
A tapestry of glee,
In twilight's symphony.

The Joyful Canvas

With colors bold and bright,
We paint our dreams in light.
Each brushstroke tells a tale,
Of joy that will not pale.

In swirls of vibrant hue,
We find a world anew.
With laughter as our guide,
In creativity, we bide.

On this canvas we explore,
Unbound by any shore.
Together, side by side,
In joy, we take our stride.

With every hue we mix,
Life's palette gently clicks.
Creating joy with ease,
A masterpiece that frees.

Sunkissed Whimsy

In gardens filled with cheer,
The sun draws us so near.
Laughter dances in the breeze,
As we sway like joyful trees.

With every twirl and spin,
New adventures can begin.
Whimsy fills the golden air,
As we wander without care.

Beneath the sky so blue,
We find the light anew.
With every joyful song,
We know where we belong.

In the warmth of the day,
All worries fade away.
Sunkissed and full of glee,
In this moment, we are free.

The Euphoria of Togetherness

In laughter, hearts entwine,
A melody divine,
With every fleeting glance,
We dance this cherished chance.

Through trials, side by side,
In love, we take the ride,
With hands held tight and true,
The world feels bright and new.

In dreams, our spirits soar,
A bond we can't ignore,
Together, we shall rise,
Beneath the endless skies.

In moments shared and small,
We find our every call,
Together, we create,
A joy that's truly great.

Radiant Reflections in Still Waters

Beneath the willow tree,
The lake reflects the spree,
Where ripples tell a tale,
Of whispers soft and frail.

The colors burst and blend,
As daylight starts to end,
Each wave a fleeting dream,
Lost in the silver gleam.

As dusk begins to chase,
The sun's warm, gentle face,
The stars begin their show,
In twilight's softened glow.

In silence, beauty calls,
The evening softly sprawls,
In stillness, hearts will find,
The peace that calms the mind.

Enchanted Moments Under Starlit Skies

Beneath the shimmering dome,
We find our hearts a home,
With wishes tossed on high,
And dreams that freely fly.

Each twinkle sparks a tale,
As shadows softly pale,
In every whispered wish,
A moment pure and blissed.

The moon casts silver light,
Transforming dark to bright,
In gentle breezes' tune,
We sway beneath the moon.

With every starry sigh,
We let our spirits fly,
Together, only us,
In magic, we entrust.

Embracing Sweet Serendipity

In chance encounters bright,
We find the pure delight,
With laughter in the air,
Each moment filled with care.

A smile, a fleeting gaze,
We're lost in joyful haze,
In paths that twist and turn,
New lessons yet to learn.

The universe conspired,
In ways we've never tired,
To guide us to this meet,
In fate's poetic beat.

With hearts so open wide,
We let the world decide,
In every twist and bend,
We find a lasting friend.

Candles of Hope and Laughter

In the dim glow, shadows dance,
Whispers of joy in every chance.
Flickering flames, hearts ignite,
Moments shared, pure delight.

Laughter rises, shadows flee,
Candles glow, we are free.
Each flicker tells a tale,
Of dreams that shimmer and prevail.

Hands held tight, warmth surrounds,
Hope's embrace in joyful bounds.
With every light, a wish takes flight,
Guided softly through the night.

Together we light, together we sing,
In the warmth of love, our spirits take wing.
Among the stars, our laughter flows,
Candles of hope, forever aglow.

An Odyssey of Cheerful Dreams

Across the skies, bright colors swirl,
A tapestry of dreams unfurl.
On gentle breezes, laughter glides,
In the heart, hope abides.

Stars align in joyful schemes,
Guiding us through cheerful dreams.
Each step a story, each turn a song,
In this odyssey, we belong.

With open hearts, we brave the night,
Chasing shadows, seeking light.
Together we dance on stardust trails,
With dreams as sails, we shall not fail.

In every heartbeat, joy remains,
A treasure found through love's refrains.
In laughter's echo, our spirits rise,
To chase the dawn, where freedom lies.

The Joy of Everyday Miracles

In morning light, the world awakes,
With simple joys, our heart takes.
A bird's sweet song, a child's bright smile,
Miracles found in every mile.

The rustle of leaves in summer's sway,
Nature's wonders on full display.
In moments small, our hearts align,
Discovering magic in the divine.

From bustling streets to quiet nooks,
Every glance holds countless books.
With laughter shared over simple things,
Life's joy, like a melody, sings.

With grateful hearts, we see it clear,
The gift of life, each moment dear.
In each breath, a miracle glows,
In the joy of living, our love grows.

Whimsical Journeys of Smiles

In a world where rainbows gleam,
Every step is a playful dream.
With whimsical colors, we set sail,
Across the skies, on a vibrant trail.

Smiles exchanged in passing days,
Light the path with laughter's rays.
In every glance, a spark ignites,
Whispers of magic, pure delights.

Through fields of daisies, hearts take flight,
We dance on clouds, feeling just right.
The essence of joy in each embrace,
Whimsical journeys, a joyous chase.

With every heartbeat, we spread our cheer,
Transforming moments, drawing near.
On whimsical paths, hand in hand,
We write our stories in colors grand.

Sailing on Serene Waters

Gentle waves embrace the shore,
Under skies of azure blue.
Sails unfurl, we wander more,
With every breath, the world feels new.

The horizon calls, a beacon bright,
A journey where the heart takes flight.
In moments still, we find our peace,
As time slows down, our worries cease.

Reflections dance upon the sea,
A canvas vast, wild and free.
Each ripple tells a story grand,
Of dreams that drift from hand to hand.

So let us sail on tranquil tides,
Where love and hope forever bides.
In every heartbeat, joy sings loud,
Among the waves, we feel so proud.

Harmonies of Hope

Soft whispers weave through the air,
A melody of tender grace.
Moments shared, we rise and care,
In each embrace, we find our place.

Through shadows deep, we find the light,
A symphony of faith unfolds.
Hand in hand, we hold on tight,
With every note, our story holds.

The dawn breaks with a gentle glow,
Promises dance on morning's dew.
Through every laugh, through every woe,
Harmonies of hope, forever true.

Together we sing, hearts entwined,
In this chorus, love is kind.
For every challenge, we will cope,
Bound by the threads of endless hope.

Dance of Delighted Hearts

In twilight's glow, our spirits soar,
With laughter sweet, we come alive.
Every step, we crave for more,
As joy ignites, our souls thrive.

A playful breeze stirs up the night,
Stars above twinkle like our dreams.
Together lost in sheer delight,
We flow like water, or so it seems.

In the rhythm, our worries fade,
With every twirl, we shed our cares.
A dance of hearts, unafraid,
In the magic, the moment fares.

So let us sway, let spirits shine,
In this embrace, our hearts align.
With every pulse, we feel the art,
As life unfolds, a dance of hearts.

Whispers of Serene Laughter

In quiet glades where shadows play,
Whispers echo, soft and sweet.
Laughter dances, light as day,
With every chuckle, we feel complete.

The world slows down, a precious gift,
In simple joy, our hearts unite.
Through gentle smiles, our spirits lift,
Together we bask in pure delight.

Nature sings in joyous streams,
As sunlight spills on mossy ground.
In these moments, we weave our dreams,
Where love and laughter can be found.

So let us cherish each fleeting sigh,
In whispers deep, our souls take flight.
With every giggle, we can cry,
In serene laughter, our hearts ignite.

Gloriously Free: The Art of Embracing Life

With open hearts, we dance and sing,
In every moment, joy we bring.
The world around, a canvas wide,
Embracing life, we take the ride.

Through storms and sun, we find our way,
In simple joys, we seize the day.
With laughter bright, we chase the light,
In freedom's arms, our spirits take flight.

Each challenge faced, a lesson learned,
In every turn, our passions burned.
Together strong, the path we tread,
In love and grace, our hearts are fed.

So here we stand, both bold and free,
In unity, our souls agree.
Let's celebrate this gift of life,
With open arms and hearts, no strife.

A Celebration of Sunsets and Smiles

The sun dips low, a golden hue,
As twilight whispers, skies turn blue.
With every smile, warmth we share,
In peaceful moments, love is rare.

Each sunset paints a story bright,
In colors rich, we find delight.
Together, under skies ablaze,
We gather close, lost in the gaze.

With laughter ringing through the night,
In simple joys, our spirits light.
A celebration, hearts align,
In every glance, our souls entwine.

So let us cherish every glow,
A tapestry of light to show.
In sunsets rich, and smiles so wide,
Together, on this joyful ride.

The Jewel of Contented Souls

In quiet moments, peace we find,
A treasure rare, a gentle mind.
With gratitude, our hearts embrace,
The beauty found in simple space.

In laughter shared, in kindness sown,
The seeds of joy become our own.
Through trials faced, we bloom and grow,
In every heart, a radiant glow.

So hold onto the joy we weave,
In every moment, we believe.
The jewel of souls, so pure and bright,
In unity, we shine the light.

Together, let our spirits soar,
In love and peace, forevermore.
The jewel of life, a bond that's whole,
In harmony, we find our soul.

Melodies of Euphoria

Whispers of joy in the breeze,
Notes of laughter dance with ease.
Sunset hues paint the sky,
As dreams take wing and fly.

Hearts entwined in sweet embrace,
Time slows down in this place.
Every moment sings a tune,
Beneath the watchful moon.

The stars join in the song,
Guiding us, where we belong.
In this world, we lose all fear,
For love's melody is clear.

Let the rhythm lead the way,
In the light of a new day.
Together, we rise and soar,
In euphoria, forevermore.

Dances of the Heart

Underneath the silver glow,
Hearts entwined, we move slow.
Each step whispers tales we share,
In this moment, nothing compares.

The music swells, our spirits rise,
Lost in the depth of our eyes.
Rhythm flows through every beat,
As we sway, the world feels complete.

In a dance, we find our voice,
With every spin, we rejoice.
Together, we chase the light,
In harmony, holding tight.

Through the night, we won't depart,
For this dance is from the heart.
In every turn, we create art,
In this beautiful dance, we start.

Laughter in Bloom

Petals open, colors bright,
Laughter blooms, pure delight.
Sunshine spills on vibrant days,
Nature dances in warm rays.

Echoes of giggles fill the air,
Joyful moments, memories rare.
In the garden of our dreams,
Life is sweeter than it seems.

With each chuckle, spirits rise,
Cascading like joyful skies.
Together under skies so blue,
In this laughter, we renew.

Let the world hear our cheer,
In this moment, love is near.
With every smile, we unmoor,
In laughter, we live for sure.

Echoes of Exultation

In the valley, joy resounds,
Echoes dance in leaps and bounds.
Voices rise, and spirits soar,
In exultation, we implore.

Every heartbeat sets the tone,
Together, we are never alone.
In the sunlight, shadows flee,
Life's a festival, wild and free.

Let the chorus fill the air,
Unity in every prayer.
In this moment, hearts ignite,
Finding peace in shared delight.

With each cheer, we find our way,
In exultation, we shall stay.
Together, we'll forever weave,
In echoes that we believe.

The Spark of Infinite Happiness

In the dawn's gentle light, we arise,
With dreams in our hearts, we touch the skies.
Every laugh shared is a treasure,
A moment captured, pure pleasure.

Holding hands beneath the wide trees,
Whispers of love carried by the breeze.
In every heartbeat, joy amplifies,
Life's sweet rhythm, a grand surprise.

Amid the shadows, hope softly glows,
Radiating warmth, as light bestows.
A dance of colors, vibrant and true,
Infinite happiness shining through.

As stars twinkle in the night's embrace,
Each memory we create, a warm place.
With every sunrise, our spirits ignite,
Together we shine, a beautiful light.

Cascade of Bright Moments

Moments cascade like a river's flow,
Each drop glistening, putting on a show.
A blend of laughter, a sprinkle of tears,
Painting our canvas through all the years.

In the quiet glow of twilight's kiss,
We find the treasures we can't dismiss.
With every heartbeat, the colors evolve,
In this dance of life, we all revolve.

Leaping through puddles, dancing in rain,
Chasing the sun, forgetting our pain.
A cascade of bright, ephemeral sights,
Moments that linger, pure delights.

Together we paint our skies so blue,
Each brushstroke a memory, old and new.
In every sparkle, a story we find,
A cascade of moments that forever bind.

Ethereal Laughter in the Breeze

Ethereal laughter floats through the air,
Dancing on whispers, light and fair.
Like petals of blossoms, soft and bright,
It fills the world with pure delight.

In the golden glow of the afternoon,
Laughter twinkles like bright silver moon.
A melody carried from heart to heart,
Binding us close, never apart.

With every giggle, the shadows fade,
A tapestry woven, love on parade.
In breezy moments, our spirits align,
Ethereal laughter, a sweet sign.

Each joke shared beneath the vast sky,
Wings of joy let our spirits fly.
With laughter's embrace, we are set free,
In this dance of life, just you and me.

Serendipity's Sweet Song

As the sun breaks through the clouds above,
Serendipity whispers tales of love.
In unexpected moments, joy unfolds,
A sweet serenade, a story told.

Through alleys we wander, discovering dreams,
Life paints its canvas with vibrant themes.
In the soft rustle of leaves that sing,
Each note weaves magic, a wondrous thing.

With open hearts, we embrace the now,
Letting go of worries, learning how.
Serendipity dances in twilight's glow,
A symphony played in ebb and flow.

With every chance taken, we find our way,
In serendipitous moments, we sway.
Life's melody swells, a beautiful throng,
Together we sing serendipity's song.

Embracing the Radiance

In morning's glow we find our way,
The golden hues invite the day.
With open arms, our hearts align,
Embracing warmth, the sun will shine.

The whispers of the gentle breeze,
Dance through branches, stir the leaves.
Each ray of light a tender touch,
A promise that we love so much.

With every dawn, new dreams arise,
We chase the light beneath the skies.
In every shadow, hope remains,
Radiance flows through joys and pains.

So let us bask in the sublime,
And find the magic in our time.
Together, through this bright expanse,
We'll write our song, our heartfelt dance.

Wings of Lightness

In a world where worries fade,
We learn to soar, unafraid.
With wings of light, we take our flight,
Into the vast and starry night.

Through skies of blue and clouds so white,
We leave behind our earthly plight.
With every gust that lifts us high,
Our spirits dance, unlimited sky.

Like feathers drifting on the breeze,
We move with grace, with such ease.
Embrace the joy of pure release,
In lightness, find our sweet increase.

Together joined, we'll never tire,
Boundless souls that soar higher.
In unity, we touch the stars,
Wings of lightness, free from scars.

The Blissful Canvas

With every brush, the colors blend,
A tapestry that knows no end.
In shades of love, joy paints the scene,
A blissful canvas, serene and clean.

The strokes of laughter fill the air,
In every corner, warmth we share.
Vibrant hues of dreams take flight,
Creating depth within the light.

Let's splash our hopes in vivid tones,
Embracing all, the heart's true bones.
With every layer, life unfolds,
A tale of memories gently told.

So gather round, let's make it bright,
Together crafting pure delight.
In this masterpiece, we belong,
A blissful canvas, a heart's song.

Freckles of Cheer

Freckles dance upon the skin,
Like constellations, bright within.
Each spot a story, hidden grace,
A patchwork of a smiling face.

In laughter's echo, joy takes flight,
With every grin, the world's delight.
Freckles sprinkle happiness wide,
In the sunshine, we abide.

So let your spirit shine and glow,
With freckles of cheer, let kindness flow.
Each mark a token of our glee,
A canvas painted joyfully.

Together, we embrace our art,
Freckles telling tales from the heart.
In every laugh, a spark is clear,
Life's beautiful with freckles of cheer.

Whispers of Delight

In the quiet of the night,
Soft secrets take their flight.
Stars twinkle with a smile,
Whispers linger for a while.

Moonbeams dance upon the sea,
Caressing all in harmony.
Gentle sighs, a lullaby,
Echoes of the night sky.

In the meadows, shadows play,
Crickets sing till break of day.
Every breath, a world untold,
Whispers of delight unfold.

With the dawn, new light arrives,
Nature wakes, and joy thrives.
In every heart, a spark ignites,
A symphony of pure delights.

Radiant Moments

Golden rays peep through the trees,
Dancing leaves in the gentle breeze.
Moments glow, a warm embrace,
Life unfolds at a graceful pace.

In the garden, petals bloom,
Their fragrance chases away the gloom.
Every color tells a story,
Radiant splendor, nature's glory.

Children laugh, their joy so free,
Every heartbeat sings in glee.
Time stands still, a cherished glance,
In radiant moments, souls advance.

As the sun dips low in the west,
Hearts find peace, and minds find rest.
With every sunset's brush of gold,
Radiant moments, memories hold.

The Laughing Breeze

Through the trees, the whisper flies,
A playful touch beneath the skies.
Tickling leaves, a lively cheer,
The laughing breeze is always near.

It brushes past with joyful sighs,
Echoing laughter, nature's cries.
Swirling leaves in a merry dance,
Bringing life to every glance.

Every path it gently sweeps,
Claims the day, and softly keeps.
A gentle nudge, it stirs delight,
The laughing breeze, a pure invite.

When day turns bright to evening's hue,
It carries dreams, both old and new.
In its embrace, we find our ease,
Forever touched by the laughing breeze.

Sunlit Serenades

Golden dawn breaks through the gloom,
Shadows chase with morning's bloom.
Every ray a soft caress,
Sunlit serenades, pure happiness.

Fields awaken, colors burst,
In this warmth, our spirits thirst.
Nature sings, a vibrant tune,
Underneath the brightening moon.

Every moment, a treasure found,
In the joy that knows no bound.
Hearts aglow with sheer delight,
Sunlit serenades, day or night.

As dusk approaches, colors blend,
With twilight's grace, the day will end.
But in our hearts, the sun will stay,
In sunlit serenades, forever play.

Chasing Sunbeams

In fields of gold, the children play,
They leap and dance, come what may,
With laughter bright, they race the light,
Chasing shadows, morning's delight.

The sun dips low, the sky aglow,
Casting rays in a radiant flow,
Whispers of dreams in the summer's breeze,
Chasing sunbeams with hearts at ease.

In every corner, joy unfurls,
As magic sparkles in whirls,
They twirl and spin without a care,
Chasing sunbeams, in bliss they share.

The day will close, yet still they seek,
The warmth of light, the song they speak,
With stars above, their laughter sings,
Chasing sunbeams, on golden wings.

The Happy Tapestry

Threads of colors, woven tight,
Stories dance in pure delight,
Each stitch a memory, soft and bright,
The happy tapestry carved in light.

With every layer, laughter grows,
A quilt of friendship, love bestows,
Through storms and sun, it will survive,
A testament to dreams alive.

In gentle hands, the fabric flows,
Together woven where kindness glows,
Patterns formed in every heart,
The happy tapestry, a work of art.

As time goes by, it will not fade,
A legacy in threads conveyed,
Embracing all, it will forever be,
The happy tapestry of you and me.

Effervescent Wonders

Bubbles rise in fizzy cheer,
Magic dances, bright and clear,
With every pop, a burst of fun,
Effervescent wonders, joy begun.

In sparkling waters, dreams collide,
Moments shimmer, like a tide,
Each tiny bubble, a wish anew,
Effervescent wonders calling you.

Laughter bubbles, swirling high,
Underneath the vast, blue sky,
With friends beside, let spirits soar,
Effervescent wonders evermore.

In every sip, a taste of bliss,
Every giggle, a gentle kiss,
Life's sweet moments, floating near,
Effervescent wonders, crystal clear.

Glimmers of Gladness

In twilight's glow, soft lights appear,
Whispers of joy, they draw us near,
Each flicker shines through darkest night,
Glimmers of gladness, pure and bright.

With heartbeats dancing, shadows fade,
Where kindness blooms, hope is made,
In every smile, a spark we find,
Glimmers of gladness, intertwined.

Through storms we walk, hand in hand,
A bridge of love, like golden sand,
With dreams alight, we chase the day,
Glimmers of gladness pave the way.

As mornings wake, the world ignites,
In every heart, a thousand lights,
Together shining, life's embrace,
Glimmers of gladness, warm our space.

Open Skies and Endless Possibilities

Under vast and open skies,
Dreams take flight like birds on high.
Whispers of hope in the breeze,
Inviting hearts to roam with ease.

The horizon calls with a friendly light,
Painting the world with colors bright.
Every step, a new chance found,
In the magic where dreams abound.

Clouds drift softly, shapes create,
Moments to cherish, never too late.
The journey begins with a single spark,
Guiding us forward, lighting the dark.

In the dance of clouds we find,
Endless paths for the wandering mind.
With open skies, we rise and roam,
Finding our place, a wondrous home.

Heartfelt Laughs Beneath the Stars

Laughter dances in the night,
Under stars so pure and bright.
Whispers shared as shadows play,
In this moment, we'll stay.

Softly glowing, the moon appears,
A witness to our hopes and fears.
Each chuckle brightens the dark,
Creating joy, a vibrant spark.

Fingers intertwined in trust,
Heartfelt laughter is a must.
Memories made, forever dear,
In the closeness, we have no fear.

Beneath the heavens, we'll remain,
With every giggle, healing pain.
Together here, in love we bask,
In heartfelt laughs beneath the stars.

Twilight Tales of Simple Bliss

In twilight's glow, a gentle calm,
The world embraces, like a balm.
Soft hues blend, a painter's dream,
Where simple moments reign supreme.

Crickets sing as day departs,
We share our hopes, we share our hearts.
Under the veil of the dusky light,
Every glance feels just right.

Candles flicker, shadows play,
Telling tales of yesterday.
In every sigh, a story spins,
Crafted by the love within.

With whispered promises, we find peace,
In simple bliss, our joys increase.
As twilight wraps us in its grace,
We cherish time, our sacred space.

The Enchantment of Loving Company

In every smile, a magic found,
Loving company, joy abounds.
With every laugh, our spirits soar,
Together, we open every door.

The warmth of hearts, a soothing light,
Guiding us on this beautiful night.
In shared glances, secrets bloom,
Creating bonds that chase away gloom.

Every moment drips with gold,
In loving company, tales unfold.
With hands held tight, we face the day,
Finding strength in every way.

As stars above twinkle and wink,
In loving company, we never sink.
Surrounded by hearts that lift us high,
The enchantment of love, a sweet lullaby.

A Garden Where Laughter Blooms

In a garden where laughter blooms,
Joy dances in the fragrant rooms.
Sunlight spills on petals bright,
Each moment sparkles in pure delight.

Breezes whisper secrets sweet,
Nature's symphony is complete.
Children play in shadows cast,
Memories made, forever last.

Butterflies flit with colors bold,
Stories of wonder quietly told.
Every bloom a tale to share,
In this haven, love fills the air.

The Radiance of Boundless Gratitude

With each dawn, gratitude sings,
Embracing all the joy it brings.
Hearts open wide to morning light,
In simple moments, spirits ignite.

Waves of kindness softly flow,
A river of thanks begins to grow.
Each smile exchanged, a treasure rare,
In this world, love fills the air.

For every blessing that we find,
A tapestry of hearts aligned.
Together we stand, hand in hand,
In the radiance of gratitude, we stand.

Morning Dew of Innocent Glee

Morning dew, a sparkling sight,
Whispers secrets, soft and bright.
Children laugh, their joy is clear,
Innocent glee brings us near.

Sunrise paints the sky in gold,
Tales of wonder now unfold.
Dreams awaken, fresh and new,
In this moment, hearts renew.

Nature's beauty, pure and true,
Every petal kissed by dew.
Innocence wrapped in the morn,
A day of marvels just reborn.

Harmony in the Dances of Life

In the silence, rhythms play,
Harmony guides us on our way.
Footsteps echo, soft and sound,
In love's embrace, we are found.

Twists and turns, the dance unfolds,
Each moment precious, each story told.
Together swaying, hearts in sync,
In the flow, we pause and think.

Life's great ballet, through joy and strife,
We find our peace in the dance of life.
In every challenge, in every cheer,
Harmony whispers, love is near.

A Symphony of Smiles

In the morning light we greet,
With laughter dancing in the street,
Each face a canvas, bright and free,
A joyful tune in harmony.

Whispers of love in the breeze,
Eyes sparkling like the autumn leaves,
A symphony playfully unfolds,
A melody of stories told.

With every chuckle heard aloud,
We gather as a cheerful crowd,
In this moment, hearts align,
Creating magic, pure and fine.

So let us share this gift of cheer,
Embracing joy we hold so dear,
In unity, let laughter rise,
A boundless symphony of smiles.

Petals of Happiness

Softly falling from the trees,
Whispers carried by the breeze,
Petals dance upon the ground,
In their beauty, joy is found.

Each bloom a burst of color bright,
A canvas painted with delight,
With fragrant notes that fill the air,
Moments cherished, love to share.

As seasons change and blossoms grow,
We gather petals, row by row,
In every hue, a story spun,
A tapestry of warmth and fun.

So let them fill our hearts with grace,
These tiny tokens we embrace,
In nature's art, we'll find our way,
Petals of happiness each day.

The Sparkling Dawn

As night gives way to morning light,
The world awakens, pure and bright,
With every drop of dew that gleams,
The dawn unfolds in vivid dreams.

Golden rays embrace the earth,
Bringing promise, joy, and mirth,
A canvas painted in pastel hues,
Each moment fresh with morning's muse.

Birds begin their cheerful song,
As daylight stretches, moves along,
With every heartbeat, hope is reborn,
In the embrace of the sparkling dawn.

A brand new chance, a chance to start,
With wonders waiting to impart,
In each sunrise, magic sings,
The sparkling dawn, a gift it brings.

Glistening Dreams

In twilight's hush, dreams start to weave,
Stories dance, and hearts believe,
Whispers glisten in the night,
Guiding souls to take their flight.

Stars above, a twinkling guide,
Through shimmering paths we glide,
Each wish a spark, each thought a beam,
Creating worlds from glistening dreams.

In shadows deep, our hopes arise,
Painting futures in the skies,
As gentle breezes softly sigh,
Our aspirations learn to fly.

So let us soar on silver streams,
Embracing all these glistening dreams,
Together hand in hand we'll turn,
To brighter stars for which we yearn.

Embrace of the Golden Hour

As the sun dips low, it paints the sky,
Shadows grow long as day bids goodbye.
Golden rays dance on the tranquil sea,
In this warm embrace, I feel so free.

Moments linger, time starts to slow,
Whispers of dusk in a gentle glow.
Colors blend like dreams in the fading light,
Wrapped in this magic, the world feels right.

Birds sing softly their evening tune,
Underneath the gaze of a silver moon.
Each heartbeat echoes with the night's sweet air,
In the golden hour, I find my prayer.

Stars awaken in the velvet sky,
Promises of night as the sun says goodbye.
Holding on tight to this fleeting scene,
In the golden embrace, I feel serene.

A Journey Through Blissful Meadows

In the heart of spring, where flowers bloom,
Fields stretch wide, dispelling gloom.
Butterflies flit from petal to petal,
Whispers of joy in each gentle settle.

Sunlight trickles through the leafy green,
A dance of shadows in the serene.
Each step taken is soft and light,
Nature's canvas, pure delight.

Hills roll gently beneath the vast sky,
Clouds drift lazily, as time floats by.
Fragrant breezes carry laughter near,
In this haven where dreams appear.

With every stride, the spirit sings,
A melody soft, on the wind that brings.
In blissful meadows, I roam at ease,
Lost in the beauty, my soul finds peace.

Kaleidoscope of Merriment

Colors swirl in a vibrant dream,
Laughter sparkles like a flowing stream.
Joy paints the world with brushes bright,
In this kaleidoscope, hearts take flight.

Children dance in the golden sun,
Playful moments, laughter spun.
Every corner holds a treasure rare,
In the tapestry of memories we share.

Rainbows arch across the vaulted sky,
Whispers of wonder as shadows fly.
In every heartbeat, a song to play,
Kaleidoscope visions, we chase the day.

Time may sway in its endless flow,
But in our hearts, the colors glow.
With every glance, we rewrite the scene,
In this dance of life, we are seen.

Bubbles of Lighthearted Wonder

Floating high on a summer breeze,
Bubbles shimmer in the golden trees.
Each one carries a dream so bright,
A dance of joy in the soft daylight.

Children giggle as they chase the spark,
In the meadow where the skies grow dark.
Popping laughter fills the air around,
In this sacred moment, magic is found.

Every bubble is a wish afloat,
Carried gently like a cozy boat.
Chasing moments, not a care in sight,
In the world of wonder, hearts take flight.

As the sun sets on this playful scene,
Bubbles burst, yet the joy stays keen.
In the light of wonder, we always stay,
Bubbles of laughter guide our way.

The Sparkle of Shared Laughter

In the garden of dreams, we twinkle bright,
Voices like chimes, dancing in the light.
Every chuckle whispers, secrets that soar,
Binding our hearts, forever we'll explore.

Under the stars, we gather and play,
Moments of joy, chasing worries away.
With laughter as lanterns, we find our way,
A treasure of memories, come what may.

Every smile a spark, igniting the night,
A symphony woven, pure and delight.
Together we weave this beautiful art,
In the tapestry of love, we each play a part.

So let echoes linger, let the world hear,
The magic that flows when you hold me near.
In the sparkle of laughter, we find our place,
A dance of our spirits, in joyous embrace.

Unraveling the Threads of Happiness

Each thread we weave, a story untold,
In colors of joy, and memories bold.
Stitch by stitch, we craft our delight,
Unraveling dreams, as day turns to night.

With whispers of hope, we nurture each seam,
Binding our hearts in a delicate dream.
Through trials and laughter, we find our way,
Unraveling the threads, come what may.

In warmth of the moment, we gather the threads,
Each knot is a memory, that love gently spreads.
Through the fabric of time, our happiness grows,
As we gather the moments, like flowers in rows.

So let us unravel, embrace every sigh,
For in these small moments, together we fly.
In the tapestry of life, we artfully stay,
Finding threads of happiness, come what may.

The Sway of Joyful Melodies

In the air, sweet notes dance, softly they sway,
Bringing warmth to our hearts at the close of the day.
Each melody blooms, with colors so bright,
In the symphony of life, we find pure delight.

With every embrace, we share in the tune,
Under the watchful eye of the gentle moon.
Together we sway, to the rhythm of cheer,
For joy in the music is better when near.

As the verses unfold, our spirits take flight,
In harmony woven, we shine with pure light.
The sway of our laughter, the echo of love,
Brings us closer, like stars up above.

So let the melodies carry us far,
In the dance of our hearts, where we'll always spar.
For in joyful harmonies, we'll forever play,
In the sway of sweet music, we'll find our way.

Hues of Warmth in Every Encounter

In each gentle glance, a story unfolds,
Colors of warmth wrapped in tales that are told.
Every meeting a canvas, painted with care,
Hues of connection linger in the air.

With laughter and kindness, we blend shades anew,
Creating a masterpiece, just me and you.
Through moments of silence, or words that we share,
In the gallery of life, our spirits lay bare.

Each hug a brushstroke, each smile a spark,
Illuminating pathways, even in the dark.
In the palette of memories, bright and profound,
We find our true colors in love's sacred ground.

So cherish each encounter, embrace every hue,
For warmth in our moments is crafted by two.
In the tapestry woven, together we stand,
In the colors of life, forever hand in hand.

The Essence of Playful Freedom

In fields of green where laughter soars,
Children dance with open doors.
Kites rise high, painting the sky,
With every twirl, the spirit flies.

Barefoot steps on dewy grass,
Chasing dreams as moments pass.
Joy spins wild in the summer air,
A tapestry of moments rare.

Whispers of wind invite the chase,
Nimble feet in a joyful race.
Each heartbeat sings a lively tune,
Under the watchful, gleaming moon.

Freedom's laugh, a timeless sound,
In every giggle, joy is found.
With arms wide open, we embrace the day,
In the essence of playful freedom, we play.

Starlight Serenade of the Heart

Under the blanket of starlit skies,
Whispers dance where silence flies.
Hearts aglow in the cool night air,
Lost in the beauty, we do not dare.

Songs of the cosmos softly weave,
Dreams take flight, hearts believe.
A symphony of twinkling lights,
Guiding souls on magical nights.

In the hush, where secrets dwell,
Starlight beckons with its spell.
Crickets strum their nightly tune,
The moon smiles down, a silver boon.

Wrapped in warmth, we close our eyes,
As starlight serenades fill the skies.
In this moment, we share the art,
Transcending time, a dance of heart.

A Breeze of Unfettered Joy

A gentle breeze sweeps through the trees,
Carrying laughter with graceful ease.
Petals flutter, the world appears,
Painted in joy, dissolving fears.

Sunshine spills on the open ground,
Every moment, pure bliss is found.
Children's giggles rise and fall,
In this symphony, we heed the call.

Clouds drift lazily, soft as dreams,
Life flows freely in silver streams.
Each breath taken, vibrant and light,
In the heart of joy, we take flight.

Embracing moments without restraint,
With open hearts, we learn to paint.
Every whisper of the breeze ignites,
A tapestry of joyful delights.

Echoes of Playful Whispers

In twilight's glow, where shadows play,
Echoes whisper the end of day.
Soft giggles trace the evening air,
As stars emerge, sparkling with flair.

Hands held tight, we wander far,
Chasing dreams beneath the stars.
With every breath, a story starts,
In the echoes of our playful hearts.

Underneath this celestial dome,
Every echo feels just like home.
Stories shared with a knowing smile,
Light the path for just a while.

As night unfolds its velvet sheet,
We dance to rhythms, oh so sweet.
In the night's embrace, let's play our part,
In echoes of whispers, the joys restart.

The Art of Cheery Anticipation

In the dawn of dreams we rise,
Hopes glimmer bright in open skies.
Every moment, a gentle tease,
Whispers of joy carried by the breeze.

A canvas painted with soft hues,
Sketches of plans, a world to choose.
With laughter dragging shadows near,
Future's promise, always clear.

Tick-tock of time, a rhythm sweet,
Each heartbeat brings a new heartbeat.
The pulse of life, in happy dance,
Inviting us to take our chance.

With every smile, a spark ignites,
The art of waiting feels so right.
In eager hearts, the dreams take flight,
Anticipation, our guiding light.

Cherished Moments in Laughter's Embrace

A burst of giggles fills the air,
Moments shared are beyond compare.
Each laugh a treasure, brightly spun,
In the arms of joy, we're always young.

Echoes linger, memories weave,
In laughter's warmth, we truly believe.
A tapestry rich, colors unite,
Binding our hearts with pure delight.

With friends around, the world's aglow,
The sweetest stories, always flow.
In joy's embrace, we find our grace,
Cherished moments, our heart's true place.

Time stands still in laughter's hold,
A symphony of love, fiercely bold.
In every chuckle, a spark remains,
Forever treasured, joy sustains.

Silhouettes of Happiness at Dusk

As day departs, the colors blend,
Silhouettes dance, as night descends.
Shadows stretch, in fading light,
Whispers of joy, taking flight.

Under the stars, stories unfold,
In twilight's glow, dreams turn to gold.
Every laugh a flicker bright,
Marking our paths in the still night.

The horizon cradles our delight,
While the moon serenades the night.
Happiness drapes like a soft shawl,
Embracing the beauty of it all.

In this moment, time stands still,
A canvas painted with warmth and will.
Silhouettes of happiness remain,
Forever etched in joy's sweet reign.

A Celebration of Sun-kissed Memories

Golden rays in laughter play,
Sun-kissed moments, bright as day.
With every heart, a story glows,
Moments cherished, everyone knows.

The warmth of sun, a playful tease,
Whispers through the swaying trees.
Echoes of joy melt every fear,
In memories dear, we hold them near.

Each photo shines like a radiant star,
Stories relived, no matter how far.
In golden hues, the past entwines,
A vibrant dance, where love aligns.

Together we weave our joyful tale,
In sun-kissed dreams, we set sail.
A celebration rich and warm,
In every memory, love takes form.

9 789916 881613